Contents

Acknowledgements iv

About the author v

Note on terminology vi

1 Introduction 1

2 Families with a difference: relationships within families with two or more severely disabled children 8

3 Changed circumstances : the impact on lifestyles and identity for families with two or more severely disabled children 18

4 Managing day to day 26

5 Families' experiences of outside support 33

6 Coordinating and delivering suitable services 48

7 Key messages and recommendations 56

Appendix   Research aims and methods 60

References 63

Acknowledgements

Particular thanks are due to all the families who participated in the research. Despite their busy lives, they were enthusiastic about the project and keen to share their experiences and contribute their views, often in the hope of improving understanding and support for other families in a similar position. Similarly, the commitment of the professionals who took part is much appreciated.

The support and interest of the Family Fund Trust and permission to use their database is gratefully acknowledged.

The Joseph Rowntree Foundation has supported the project financially and offered valuable advice throughout, firstly through Claire Benjamin and, latterly, Emma Stone. The project advisory group has provided continuous encouragement and helped to highlight the relevance of the project. Robina Shah was an invaluable colleague in her contribution to the fieldwork and following discussions.

Ian Sinclair at the Social Work Research and Development Unit has provided initial and continuing support, Helen Jacobs has managed the budget and other administration of the project and colleagues at the Social Policy Research Unit, especially Dot Lawton and Teresa Frank, have provided assistance which has contributed to the successful completion of the project. My sincere thanks to them all.

Rosemary Tozer
September 1999

At the Double

Supporting families with two or more severely disabled children

Rosemary Tozer

SUPPORTED BY

JR
JOSEPH
ROWNTREE
FOUNDATION

NATIONAL
CHILDREN'S
BUREAU

The National Children's Bureau (NCB) works to identify and promote the well-being and interests of all children and young people across every aspect of their lives.

It encourages professionals and policy makers to see the needs of the whole child and emphasises the importance of multidisciplinary, cross-agency partnerships. The NCB has adopted and works within the UN Convention on the Rights of the Child.

It collects and disseminates information about children and promotes good practice in children's services through research, policy and practice development, membership, publications, conferences, training and an extensive library and information service.

Several Councils and Fora are based at the NCB and contribute significantly to the breadth of its influence. It also works in partnership with Children in Scotland and Children in Wales and other voluntary organisations concerned for children and their families.

The **Joseph Rowntree Foundation** has supported this project as part of its programme of research and innovative development projects, which it hopes will be of value to policy makers and practitioners.

The views expressed in this book are those of the authors and not necessarily those of the National Children's Bureau or the Joseph Rowntree Foundation.

ISBN 1 900990 53 9

Published by National Children's Bureau Enterprises Ltd, 8 Wakley Street, London EC1V 7QE

National Children's Bureau Enterprises Ltd is the trading company for the National Children's Bureau (Registered Charity number 258825).

Typeset by LaserScript Ltd, Mitcham, Surrey CR4 4NA

Printed and bound in the United Kingdom by Redwood Books, Trowbridge, Wiltshire BA14 8RN

About the author

Rosemary Tozer originally trained as a social worker, working in probation, for an innovative fostering project and in social work training. More recently she has undertaken research into user involvement and older people, the siblings of disabled children and the research on which this book is based. She is based at the University of York. Two of her three children are severely disabled.

Note on terminology

The appropriate terminology to use when writing about disability is a much debated issue amongst researchers and those whose lives are affected by disability. However, it is agreed to be of paramount importance that the terms used do not have negative connotations or depersonalise those to whom they refer. In line with the social model of disability which is supported by the Joseph Rowntree Foundation, a distinction has been made in this report between *impairment* which refers to individual, often medical, conditions and *disability*, a generic term which refers to the social disadvantage experienced by those with impairments. However, the term 'impairments' is often not used by practitioners, policy makers and parents, and also some conditions are generally referred to as physical or learning 'disabilities'. Thus, whilst aiming to support the language of the social model of disability, other commonly understood terms are used occasionally within this report.

The term 'severely disabled', as used in this research report, is taken to mean significant impairments such as severe learning disabilities, multiple impairments, and impairments related to specifically diagnosed conditions, such as autism and cerebral palsy. The sample of 24 families who participated in the qualitative part of the project were mostly drawn from the Family Fund Trust database. The Trust helps families where the child/children are 'very severely disabled', but prefers to consider the impact of a specific condition on the individual(s) and the family, rather than assuming a degree of impairment associated with a particular diagnosis.

1 Introduction

The Baker Family

Clive and Sue Baker have three children: Joanne aged 15, Louise aged 12 and Adam aged nine. Both Louise and Adam have severe learning and physical disabilities, although neither a name nor a reason for their difficulties has been found. The family live on a suburban council estate in a three-bedroomed house which has been adapted to meet some of Louise's and Adam's needs with a through-floor lift. Joanne and Louise like sharing a bedroom, but it is sometimes hard for Joanne to get her homework done. This is because Louise goes to bed early, although she is often awake during the night. Clive used to be employed by a haulage company but he gave up work six years ago when the extent of Adam's difficulties became clear and Sue was having a period of ill health. They say that they both need to be at home when the children are there and to be able to take them out. They have acquired an adapted vehicle through the Motability Scheme.

Louise and Adam attend the same special school, with which their parents are pleased. They seem to like each other's company and both enjoy watching cartoons and listening to rock music. However, when Adam is unhappy, he shows this by biting his hand or hitting other people. This upsets his sisters and so, at times, the children need to be apart with one of their parents.

The family have a social worker who has arranged for Louise to stay with a single carer one weekend a month, and for Adam to stay at a residential centre one night a week. Both children attend a special playscheme in the summer holidays. Except when the children are at school, Clive and Sue find it hard to get out together. Joanne will babysit in the evenings so they can go out for an hour or so, but she finds it hard to cope if both her brother and sister need attention at the same time. Clive's parents live 50 miles away. Although Sue's family live nearby and are supportive, particularly with Joanne, they are not able to help with the care of Louise and Adam.

It is apparent that, for the Baker family, having two children with severe disabilities creates difficulties which affect everyone in the family. Some of these difficulties are experienced by families with one disabled child, whilst others are particular to those with two or more disabled children. For instance, there are times when two carers are essential. While the Baker family appreciate the help they have had from different support agencies over the years, sometimes it has been hard for them to get the help they need in bringing up their children in the way that they would like and doing things like other families. The Bakers do not know any other families with two or more disabled children and have often wondered how many there are. Their particular circumstances also raise other questions:

- How far are their experiences common to other families with two or more severely disabled children?
- Would things be more difficult or easier if the children had very different disabilities?
- How would Clive and Sue manage without Joanne's help or if there was only one parent?
- What would the differences be if the family were from a minority ethnic community with English as a second language?
- Do some parents in this situation manage to work?
- Can families with two or more disabled children be offered a complete break from caring?

The research study

In order to answer these and related questions, a programme of research was carried out at the University of York between 1997 and 1999, supported by the Joseph Rowntree Foundation. Its purpose was to find out how many families there are like the Bakers, what their circumstances are, their ways of managing and their experiences of support services. Previous research studies had included families with more than one disabled child in their sample (Green and Murton, 1993; Beresford, 1995), but only one had looked specifically at families with more than one severely disabled child (Wild and Rosenbloom, 1985).

Anecdotal evidence of practitioners working with families suggests that support agencies typically know several such families and that this is not an uncommon family structure. However, despite their presence in the community, without information about the specific situation, experiences and support needs of these families, their particular concerns could be marginalised when policies and practice guidelines are being developed and implemented.

Numbers and circumstances

The first part of the project was quantitative. For the first time, the numbers of families in the UK with two or more severely disabled children were estimated. Analysis of information on 100,000 families from the Family Fund Trust database suggested that about ten per cent of these families had more than one child with a disability or chronic illness. Further investigation indicated that in the UK up to 7,500 families have two or more *severely* disabled children, representing at least 15,000 children plus non-disabled siblings (Lawton, 1998). About half of these families had children registered with the same conditions. Details about these families from the database, together with analysis of material about 39 families from a previous study (Beresford, 1995), allowed a picture of these families to be built up and some comparisons made between their circumstances and those of families with only one disabled child. Not surprisingly, this indicated that families with two or more severely disabled children are more likely to be disadvantaged than families with one disabled child. For example, parents are less likely to be working and therefore dependent on benefits; more parents report having a disability or chronic illness themselves; families are more likely to be headed by a lone parent and less likely to be living in their own home. There were also indications that families with more than one severely disabled child had particular difficulties in accessing support, both from relatives and from service agencies (Tozer, 1999).

Research methods

The second stage of the project, on which this report is based, has comprised detailed qualitative work with 24 families in the North of England. The sample of families who took part was drawn from the Family Fund Trust database, and tried to include as much diversity as possible in the conditions and profiles of the children and their family circumstances. The quantitative analysis outlined above and other recent research (Chamba and others, 1999) has indicated that there is an increased incidence of families with more than one disabled child in South Asian communities. Six families were therefore specifically recruited from Pakistani communities, both to ensure their representation and to afford an understanding of the similarities and the differences between their experiences and those of white families. Robina Shah, a researcher fluent in Urdu and Punjabi, worked with these families and the material from her fieldwork has been integrated into this report. It is clear that caring for two or more severely disabled children is likely to be a very similar experience for families across ethnic communities and it is important that this commonality is understood. However, it is also apparent from the accounts of the small number of South Asian families who took part in this study that access to suitable services and support is not only likely to be much reduced, but also compounded by language barriers and cultural misunderstandings.

Through direct contact with all 24 families it was possible to explore key questions raised by the findings of the first quantitative stage. Why, for instance, did only half the families have a parent in employment? And why can it be difficult for families to receive the support that they want?

This second qualitative stage of the project adopted a 'whole-family' perspective. Recent approaches to understanding and supporting families with disabled children have recognised the need to include the whole family (*The Children Act 1989*; Carpenter, 1997). Likewise, research methods were devised which, as far as possible, would enable all family members to take part in the research. These methods involved a mixture of interviews and time spent with the family informally both observing what happened at home and getting to know the children. Some child-friendly materials were developed to assist the children's contribution (see the Appendix for more details of the research methods). Typically, families were visited on three occasions, although this varied between two and five contacts. Each family was asked to suggest a key professional or support agency with whom they had had contact, and these people were then interviewed either in person or by telephone.

The researchers

The main researcher and author of this report is herself a parent of two severely disabled sons. She had often wondered how many other families were in a similar position and whether many of the difficulties they faced were related to having *two* children with considerable support needs. Support services seemed designed for mothers with one disabled child and were often blinkered about the involvement or needs of other family members. The researcher who worked with the South Asian families who took part has a sibling with a physical disability.

Researchers frequently have personal experiences that are relevant to the subject they are studying. There is always a danger that their own assumptions can lead them to ignore important aspects of a topic that seem too familiar to be noteworthy or are out of the range of their own experience. The research methods employed in this study, with several contacts with each family, were intended to make this less likely. Research skills should also ensure that personal experiences can be an advantage to a researcher. Certainly, the author found that being a parent herself seemed to give credibility with families and afforded ideas about the important themes in framing the research questions at the start of the study.

The policy context

Recently, several government reviews and initiatives have related to 'children in need' and their carers, with associated funding for extra local provision becoming available. The *Quality Protects* (Department of Health, 1998) initiative focuses on the management of children's services, including those for children with disabilities, and requires the development and implementation of inter-agency strategies and partnerships at local level. *Caring About Carers: A national strategy about carers* (Department of Health, 1999) emphasises the need for carers to have short breaks and opportunities to combine caring with paid work. As will become apparent through reading this report, issues of service coordination, short-term care and employment are particularly important to families with two or more severely disabled children.

Equally, a range of legislation, such as the Children Act 1989, the Carers' Act 1995 and the Disability Discrimination

Act 1996, provides opportunities to help disabled children and their families. This legislation can be drawn on by agencies to support families, including those with more than one disabled child, once their needs are understood.

A recent Government report, *Removing Barriers for Disabled Children* (Social Services Inspectorate, 1998), suggested that the biggest barriers were frequently caused by organisational attitude, so that child protection issues, for example, were often ignored in relation to disabled children. The inspection also noted that, in contrast to their non-disabled peers, disabled children were usually neither worked with directly, nor given choices, nor offered independent advocacy. The inspection concluded that every social services department needs to have a 'champion' for disabled children to ensure a greater awareness of their needs. This 'champion' would ensure a planned programme of support for these children and their families, enhanced by good communication between agencies, coordinated assessment and specialist workers.

In the light of these policy and practice initiatives, this report about a particular group of families who are likely to have extra support needs is timely. It is hoped that it will inform current debates and service planning and add to existing knowledge about families with disabled children.

Plan of the report

Through analysis of the material collected from families with two or more disabled children, it is clear that they want professionals to understand what family life is actually like for them and how they manage the care of their children day to day. This is because they would like service providers and professionals to see things through their eyes and to take account of their particular circumstances, so that what is provided is based on an understanding of the whole family's experiences, priorities and preferences.

The report has been written and ordered to try and reflect this wish. To start, Chapter 2 describes the effects on relationships, both positive and negative, of being part of a family where two or more of the children have severe disabilities. In Chapter 3, the implications for the lifestyles and choices of all family members are considered, and also how families see themselves in the light of their differences from others. How dual caring is managed by the family is the focus of Chapter 4, leading to an examination of the kinds of support that families do receive, or would like to, in Chapter 5. Chapter 6 looks at some of the organisational issues that are relevant to service providers in responding to the needs of families in an appropriate and coordinated way. Specific questions aimed at professionals are posed at the end of each chapter, and the report finishes by summarising the key messages for policy and practice.

Many quotes from the participants in the study are included in this report. Generally, these have been selected because an individual's words bring to life experiences and issues that are common to many others. For this reason, and to protect anonymity, the quotes have not been specifically attributed in a way which would allow the speaker to be identified. Similarly, it has not been spelt out which ethnic group individuals are from, although this may be apparent from a first name, except when a point is being made about particular experiences amongst one group of families.

Note: All names have been changed.

2 Families with a difference: relationships within families with two or more severely disabled children

This chapter looks at how the disabilities of two or more children make a difference to the relationships between all those in the immediate family, including the disabled and non-disabled children, how they respond to these differences and how they view family life.

Mothers and fathers

The effects of caring for a severely disabled child on marriages and partnerships has generally been measured by looking at patterns of lone parenthood and partnership breakdown. Analysis of the Family Fund Trust database showed that families with two or more disabled children are more likely to be headed by a lone parent than those with one disabled child; 28 per cent compared to 22 per cent (Lawton, 1998). In three out of the 24 families who took part in this study, lone mothers were separated or divorced from the father of their children. A further four mothers had new partners. Amongst these seven mothers, three felt strongly that their children's disabilities had contributed to the breakdown of their first marriage, and that diagnosis of a second disabled child had been the last straw:

> I think he was only at home for six months [after the diagnosis] before he decided to take a job away. He's never been able to deal with it at all.

Another mother suggested that the stigma of disability had been the main difficulty for the children's father:

> He wanted out because he couldn't cope, his parents didn't want to accept that there was a disability in the family. When Laura was ill, he just didn't want to know. ... We found out later, much later on, that he'd not actually told people at work that we had

Laura and Stephen, which is really sad. He just said, you know, 'We have two children, Michael and Claire'.

In one family, it had been the problem of handling difficult behaviour and disagreements about this, a cause of tension in other families too, which had led to the father moving out of the home, although he visited several times a week. This arrangement had eased the tension and allowed him still to be an active father. The mother in this family felt that her husband had long felt left out because of the prolonged dependency of her two sons.

Other mothers said that their relationship had been breaking down anyway for other reasons and, in some cases, had done so before the children's difficulties were recognised. Nevertheless, several couples talked about the extra strain put on their partnership. This was particularly the case if neither parent was working in order to manage the care of two disabled children:

> I mean, every relationship's got its ups and downs, and with the added pressures we've got. Especially like Keith had to give up work, so basically we're with each other 24 hours a day. Considering all that, we must get on pretty well.

Being at home did allow fathers and stepfathers to play a greater part with the children and domestic tasks and have more contact with professionals, such as teachers, health or social workers. Couples could then feel that they were involved in a joint enterprise. Although this could isolate them from other networks, some said that it had brought them closer:

> The children's difficulties have made our relationship stronger. We are more considerate towards each other, and a lot more tolerant of each other.

In the families where this worked, there was an expectation that fathers would play an equal part in the extra tasks of caring. This often amounted to one parent caring for each child. If this did not happen, resentment could build up:

> I mean, physio, there's two of them and it does take a while and I mean it can be harder, two kids on the wedge as opposed to having one. But he would just sit and watch me do it, he wouldn't help or anything.

This mother resented her husband's ability to get out of the situation, which she felt was denied to her:

> I do almost everything, my husband tries to help but he soon gets fed up with the noise in the house. He goes off to his friend's house. Really, if I think about it, I can't cope without the help my husband does give me, but I would like to go out and visit my friend's house.

It would appear that a few fathers found it difficult to assume an ongoing active involvement with their children and their care. Support specifically for fathers was absent and some felt that they missed out on what was available because professionals called at the house when they were out at work. One father described how the paediatrician had addressed him rather than his wife when they were told of their children's disabilities, but subsequently he had felt unsupported:

> It's all on the mother. Because you're supposed to be out here being the breadwinner and what have you ... really there's nothing for fathers and there's nobody to explain anything.

However, in the majority of families where fathers or stepfathers were able to play a significant part, this seemed to benefit everyone and generally strengthened the parents' partnership. For those mothers who had new partners, this more active involvement meant improved support, although the stepfathers themselves considered they were 'only doing what any father would do':

> He takes them everywhere, he doesn't bother, he just takes them off and, you know, they're accepted. ... It's a relief, really, because he's always shown that he wants to care for them.

Parents and children

Whatever their level of disability or the difficulties that their children's impairments might create for the family, parents' affection for and pride in their children was visible and tangible in nearly all the families who took part in the study. As other researchers have found (Beresford, 1994; Bennett and others, 1996), positive and reciprocal relationships are a vital part of the caring equation. One father said:

> I know there's something wrong with them but to me they're our kids. I see 'em as being all right.

Parents found it supportive and affirming if children were liked and perhaps popular at school. Many talked proudly of

their children's attributes, their attractiveness, their personalities or their achievements, be it managing to survive so
long, writing their name, or an act of kindness. Signs of
progress, however small or imperceptible to others, were
celebrated. The two adoptive families in the sample, in
particular, emphasised the rewards that had come from
creating a family of this structure. They realised, however,
that these rewards were often incomprehensible to outsiders.

Feelings of unfairness were also common, with questions of
'Why them?' or 'Why us?', as parents tried to make sense of
their situation and their children's differences. However, most
parents soon became caught up in trying to get the best
services for their children and encourage them to achieve
positive things. Although this effort could be all-consuming,
parents also recognised the rewards in their situation and
that other aspects of their lives had their downside.

> People seem to think when you've got two disabled children, they
> don't see that they bring you a lot of pleasure, you have a lot of
> happiness. If you're fed up, people look at you as if it's them. You
> get fed up of other things as well, don't you?

In their accounts, parents described their children's 'normal-
ity', for example, saying things like, 'That's teenagers all over',
but they were also acutely aware of the differences. Some
parents, particularly those with no other children, commented
on what they thought their children would never be able to do
and the sadness they sometimes felt on seeing other families
with non-disabled children, as expressed by this father:

> You see them doing things with them, going to the cinema, things
> like that. But you just get on with it. It's no good wishing 'I wish
> you could do this, I wish you could do that'. One thing, I always
> wanted a son, always wanted to take him to the park and have a
> game of football with him. Like if the nephews are here, the
> park's just across the way there. I couldn't really say, 'Come on,
> let's go and have a game of football', it just wouldn't feel right.

Nearly half the families who took part in the study also had
non-disabled children. These siblings could bring a welcome
sense of 'ordinary' family life and, once they were at school,
contact with mainstream networks that were often out of the
reach of the disabled children. Even so, parents tended to worry
that the lives of their non-disabled children were constrained,
and often disrupted, by the impairments of their siblings. This
mother commented about her two teenage daughters:

They can't have friends back here because they're so over the top with them, the two little ones.

A few parents said they had been too preoccupied with the disabled children to notice the effects on their other sons or daughters. More often, parents were concerned to give their other children enough attention and not to put too much responsibility onto them, particularly if they were the only non-disabled child in the family:

I have a lad of 14 and I think they tend to get left out because it's 'Can you look at this, Mum?' But I'm too busy, I've got to do this, I'm changing Emma or I'm changing Katie or I've got to feed one of them.

Inevitably, sometimes parents had to rely on the availability of brothers and sisters to help, for example in the school holidays, when only limited support was likely to be available from service providers. This was particularly the case within the six South Asian families who took part in the study, none of whom were receiving any support from social services.

Brothers and sisters

The composition of these families meant that every child, including the disabled children themselves, was also the brother or sister of at least one disabled child. This allowed or required some of the disabled children to have a caring role in relation to one or more of their siblings. Sometimes, this involved looking out for a brother or sister at school, as might happen in any sibling relationship.

One mother described how her son had advocated for his twin brother:

Before Alex was ill last year, he used to look after Chris all the time. If they took Chris to the nurse at school, he used to go down in his electric wheelchair and say, 'What are you doing? Write it down to tell my mum'.

In some families, a disabled young person may be playing a crucial role in helping to care for a more disabled or younger sibling: 'If we hadn't got Simon now, we couldn't look after Mark'.

Sometimes reciprocal help took place between disabled and non-disabled siblings as between any pair of siblings. Here, a 16-year-old boy describes his relationship with his brother aged 20 who has a physical disability:

I look after Farouk. I accompany him to the shops, help him with picking things up. ... I help Farouk and he helps me with my homework.

Compatibility between the children in the family was a positive factor which eased the situation for everyone. Having similar experiences of a disability could be supportive: 'My brother is a good listener and he helps me a lot'.

Even when children had very severe impairments, some parents described the relationship between siblings as being 'just like any brother and sister'. They felt that the companionship the children offered each other was very valuable. Some parents thought that the disabled children had a particular understanding and tolerance of each other:

They just say, 'Oh well, it's Jack' or 'Well, Jack doesn't understand properly'. So they're very ready to make excuses for him. And, you know, quite ready to help him. And often they will translate what he's trying to say.

In other families, the disabled children's personalities and behaviour were less compatible or there was a big gap between the children in terms of age or ability. Some children appeared to have very little contact with each other, particularly if social skills were affected by their impairment, as in autism. Sometimes, it was frustrating for one child if the other did not respond:

I think Ben would like to play with his brother because he enjoys rough and tumble with his dad. He actually approaches Tom, but Tom doesn't know how to deal with it.

Sometimes, parents felt obliged to separate children in different parts of the house to pursue different activities or to keep the children safe from each other:

Our house is very separated; to keep it on a quiet level, we're all in separate rooms.

The majority of parents were unable to leave the children alone together, even briefly, and two commented on the possibility of inappropriate sexual behaviour.

There was some evidence that, as they grew older, non-disabled siblings took on increased caring responsibilities. Generally, sisters and brothers expressed their love for and pride in their disabled siblings, but also their concern for them and for themselves. Here, a 16-year-old sister talks about the ways in which the time spent caring for her brother and sister affects other areas of her life:

> I've found this year and last year that I've never really met a deadline, it's always been late, and then it's not that good anyway, my homework. I find that my work has suffered 'cos my mum and dad didn't used to go out that much, but now they've started going out more.

> If I spend time with my friends, I haven't got time to do my homework and, if I do my homework, I haven't got time to see my friends and sometimes I haven't got time to do either really.

Despite these and other anxieties, only one sibling in the sample was accessing a specific service, and the others had only fleeting contact with support personnel, if at all. It was also generally the case that the disabled children tended to have indirect contact with professionals. One key worker expressed her concern that she was obliged to support both the parents and the children in a family, when it would be more appropriate for the children to have their own worker or advocate.

The wider family

The attitudes and degree of support from the extended family were also important. The reactions and contribution of grandparents were particularly significant to the families who took part in the study. Those who had found the diagnosis difficult to accept or understand were unlikely to be offering much emotional or practical support. Parents sometimes said they could only call on the grandparents 'if we're absolutely desperate'. It seemed that help that was not willingly given could be undermining and upsetting. This tended to be related to the nature of the previous relationship between parent and grandparents (Mirfin-Veitch and Bray, 1997). Understandably, the lack of support from grandparents who lived nearby was resented, especially in an emergency:

> Like a few months ago we'd all got 'flu, my mother came down [and] asked if we wanted anything from the Post Office. I said, 'Well, could you fetch Colin from school?' 'Oh no, I can't do that'. The fact was that she had to pass the school to go to and from the Post Office.

For other families, grandparents could be invaluable, often providing extra pairs of hands in a flexible way that could meet the needs of parents and children. Some had taken disabled children on holiday, or to their home to stay, and frequently came round to help and babysit regularly. Others had a particular role with non-disabled siblings. Grandparents saw themselves as both helping their children and enjoying their grandchildren:

> I mean, these two wouldn't get out if it weren't for me, for them to have a weekend on their own, so I take the two little ones.

> I never thought there'd be a problem with my mum and dad 'cos, you know, they were fine with Sarah, and he's [Harry] their grandson and he's wonderful.

In one family, both grandparents came round every morning and evening to help with their grandsons. Several parents expressed such a confidence in grandparents who helped regularly that they found hard to transfer to outside carers who usually had a more tenuous relationship with their child or children. However, the amount of practical help that grandparents could provide inevitably decreased as their energy declined with age and the children grew older. The behaviour of two older severely disabled children might be harder for them to manage and physical care also became more difficult, if children needed lifting or had fits. Thus, the help that grandparents could provide tended to become more limited at a time when the demands on parents or siblings were becoming greater.

Although recent research (Chamba and others, 1999) has indicated that families from Pakistani communities are likely to receive similar levels of support from the extended family as white families, the six South Asian mothers who took part in the study reported little help from the wider family, apart from sympathy:

> Family members feel sorry and upset, basically because they see no future for these children. Practically, they offer no support. The family offers some emotional support which isn't always helpful. It's the pity I can't stand.

In some families, support was forthcoming from other relatives, such as uncles, aunts and older cousins. However, parents did not usually expect as much help from busy relatives of the same generation and were satisfied if their children were accepted and treated the same as other nephews and nieces. Any extra support was considered to be a bonus.

Summary

Members of families with two or more severely disabled children experience and express the same range of emotions about each other as individuals in any family. In many ways, their relationships are just like those within families without severe disability with both good times and family tensions, which may or may not have anything to do with the children's disabilities.

At the same time, where there are two or more disabled children, their relationships with other family members can be very different, even though they will still be mutually satisfying and, in some cases, mutually supportive. Extra support, care and supervision are usually needed for severely disabled children. This affects everyone in the family, requiring time and attention from the whole household and often those in the wider family, too. It would appear that the extra tasks that are created are picked up, to some extent, by everyone in the family, including the disabled and non-disabled siblings. If certain family members are less able to play their part because of other demands or their disinclination, others in the family will have to increase their contribution. Thus, if one parent is absent or ill, grandparents or older siblings are likely to have a greater caring role.

This can also be an issue for families with just one disabled child if, for instance, they are headed by a lone parent. However, for families with two or more disabled children, the need for two carers is greater. The compatibility of the children is also an extra factor. Sometimes, it is the combination of the children's personalities and their differing needs, rather than their individual impairments, which is particularly difficult for them and their families to manage. This contrasts with the benefits brought by children who are generally well matched or who complement each other.

Practice points

Support agencies have traditionally concentrated their attention on disabled children and their mothers, because the mother is usually the main carer. A broader perspective is now necessary to understand the needs of the family as a whole, while encompassing individual wishes and concerns. This is not an easy balance to achieve, but it is vital if the *whole family* is to be effectively and appropriately supported.

In any agency, how can service providers:

- recognise the involvement of all family members in the care and support of disabled children;
- ensure that fathers, grandparents, and brothers and sisters are all offered their own supports;
- work directly with the children of the family to understand their experiences and views;
- try to replicate flexible informal support for those without sufficient help from the extended family or other networks?

In the next chapter, the effects of having two or more severely disabled children on the lifestyle and identity of families will be explored further.

3   Changed circumstances: the impact on lifestyles and identity for families with two or more severely disabled children

This chapter examines how families with two or more severely disabled children adapt their identities and lifestyles to accommodate their children's needs. It also looks at the access by such families to supportive networks, and the impact of public perceptions.

Not working

The quantitative analysis that constituted the first phase of the project indicated that parents of two or more severely disabled children are less likely to be in work than those with one disabled child, who are in turn much less likely to be employed, even part time, than those in the general population (Lawton, 1998). Although studies of carers generally indicate a reduction in employment (Twigg, Atkin and Perring, 1991) only seven per cent of mothers, whether single or with partners, and 51 per cent of fathers in the sample of around 7,500 families were working full or part time. This compares to figures of 12 per cent and 63 per cent of mothers and fathers of one disabled child, and 60 per cent and 80 per cent in the general population.

Within the sample of families who took part in the second qualitative phase of the project, in only a third of families was either parent working, with only one mother working part time. Among the remaining 16 families, nine parents were unable to work or would have found it harder to do so because of their own ill health or impairment. In six families, there was a clear connection between a chronic condition in a parent and the children's disabilities. Either a parent had the same condition, usually to a lesser degree, or caring had resulted in injury, the exacerbation of a pre-existing condition, or associated stress.

In addition, four fathers or stepfathers had given up work because of the requirements of the children's care, which could not be met by mothers alone. If fathers were in unskilled employment, they were barely able to earn more than the family would receive on benefits.

> He was missing out on a lot of the times, but apart from that it was really difficult for me to deal with them both. .... We actually sat down and worked it out, you know, even though we were going to be running at a loss, we thought it was worth it.

Virtually all the parents in the study said they would like to be able to work, even if part time. They said this would give them a change from their routine, allow them to get out and meet people and use and develop other abilities.

This, and other aspects of parents' relationship with employment, is in line with the findings of a research study which has highlighted the difficulties faced by parents of disabled children when trying to combine paid work and caring (Kagan, Lewis and Heaton, 1998), and the experiences collected by a national network of working parents of disabled children (*Parents at Work*, forthcoming).

Several mothers who took part in this study considered that they had developed new skills through having disabled children, which they hoped at some time to develop into work opportunities or new careers. For example, one felt that the knowledge she had acquired through her sons' physical difficulties had encouraged her to train as an aerobics teacher. Another who had been providing palliative nursing care to her son planned to complete her nursing training when he died. Others felt that their knowledge of special needs, the care system or signing had given them competencies which they would like to develop further in the future.

Currently, these parents considered it to be practically impossible to work. Aside from the loss of benefits and possible ill health among parents, it would be difficult for them to find work that fitted in with school hours and holidays, when two or more severely disabled children would need care. Frequently, two parents were needed when the children were at home, such as after school, and parents described being 'on call' from school if the children were taken ill or other difficulties arose. No parents had been offered help with child care in order to work, and support agencies apparently considered it beyond their remit to provide such help.

Here, a mother with three children with learning disabilities in a mainstream school describes the situation:

> I'd love to get a part time job but, if it was in school hours, the
> school would be ringing up saying, 'Mark's had an accident,
> Jamie's done this', so I'd be having to take time off. . . . and Jenny,
> it's only the beginning of this year that she's stopped wetting
> herself and she was eight then, so it could be another three years!

Although special schools were generally used to dealing with
such incidents, parents often felt that they had to be at the
end of a telephone in case children had fits or were suddenly
taken ill. Moreover, during the day they were expected to be
available for appointments or to help in schools (Todd and
Shearn, 1996). A few parents had acquired pagers so that they
could go shopping, but still be contactable.

> Social services got us a pager and that's been a godsend, because
> before I used to take them to school and I'd just sit in. I just
> wouldn't go anywhere, I mean, I didn't even dare go to the toilet
> in case the phone rang. It was really awful.

Nevertheless, at the time of interview, many parents
expressed their frustration that they felt unable to undertake
paid employment. Reliance on benefits meant that parents
found it hard to meet the extra costs associated with caring for
disabled children (Dobson and Middleton, 1998). They
mentioned difficulty, for example, in paying sitters or buying
special toys and equipment. Some families, including those
where one parent was working, felt that they could not afford
their own transport because of the running costs involved.
Parents with physically disabled children had usually
acquired an adapted vehicle through the Motability Scheme.

Just carers

Reductions in employment opportunities, limited social networks and the amount of time spent caring for two or more
severely disabled children tended to emphasise the parental
role. However, everyone in the family had their lives
restricted to some extent, including the disabled children.
Apart from school and occasional short-term care, the
disabled children had few opportunities to socialise and were
usually unable to go out unaccompanied. These limitations, in
turn, meant that everyone in the family spent more time with
each other at home than might be the norm.

Although usual in families with very young children, for families with two or more severely disabled children, this situation could continue indefinitely. As Todd and Shearn (1996) found, parents generally had to abandon plans for themselves in the immediate future. Several parents expressed the hope that they would not be in the same situation when they were in their seventies, although the future in five or ten years' time was something that they often preferred not to contemplate. Many parents wanted more of a life away from disability, but generally found this hard to achieve. Perhaps going to a gym or attending adult education classes for a few hours a week or an occasional pint at the pub was the best they could hope for.

> Sometimes, you sit back and think, 'Well, I ain't got a life'. ... Particularly when things have been really hard, as they have over the last few weeks, I think, 'Well, where am I going? What am I doing? What have I got that is just for me?'

Frequently, parents felt that their own identities had been submerged in their parenting and caring roles. They were seen as the parents of disabled children, a view reinforced by the demands and attitudes of the education and care systems, which negotiated with them as carers rather than as individual adults (Twigg, 1989).

> I'm known as the one who drives the red van with the kids in the wheelchairs.

Public perceptions

> We go on holiday and they say, 'Are they all yours?'!

Families frequently talked about their visibility in public, when they were out with their two disabled children. They were very sensitive to the reactions of others and generally did not welcome increased interest in the children because of their appearance or unusual behaviour. This sort of unsolicited attention could make them feel that their parenting was under scrutiny. Some parents felt they were likely to be criticised for either spoiling their children, or being too strict. They were often drawn into having to explain about the children to strangers. Some saw themselves as ambassadors for disability awareness, but it was still an irksome task.

> I think sometimes they look at me and think, 'Why can't she have a normal child?' You know, sort of thing. And I find myself explaining all the time about my children and I shouldn't have to, but I do.

A few families did report more positive responses to their children on longer acquaintance. Although comments might not have been made if the children had not had disabilities, in the following situation the children seemed to have broken the ice:

> Even in the holiday club, the [other] children accepted them, they were great. And we went swimming, you know. We got people staring and all that when we were on the beach. But we got a lot of couples coming up and talking to us and saying, 'You've got two great kids there'. You know, really nice.

Non-disabled siblings tended to be embarrassed by people staring, especially during their teens. They also worried what their friends would think when they first called at the house, even though they had usually tried to explain about their brothers' or sisters' disabilities:

> Like this friend of mine, he was a right nutter at school, he was always telling jokes ... he was really affected when he saw them ... he just seemed stunned.

Whatever the reaction of others, all family members would have preferred to do without unsolicited attention when in public and to have preserved their privacy and anonymity. Extra scrutiny increased feelings of isolation and being different.

Isolation

This feeling of separateness was a thread that ran through the lives of the families who took part in the study. They compared themselves to others without disabled children, or with just one disabled child. However rewarding their situation, they generally saw their lives as being more challenging and difficult than other families'. Sometimes, they saw themselves as practically isolated, with their need and desire to get out and visit other people made more difficult by the lack of transport or managing the children in order to do so. Sometimes, this sense of isolation was compounded by familial or cultural expectations.

There was also a separateness related to not really belonging to any particular peer group. Few families knew of others with more than one disabled child, although those who did had found this helpful. Those families who had non-disabled children or children in mainstream school could feel as though they were straddling two cultures, while being at times on the edge of both. This mother described being different within a 'normal' setting:

> There are five children with special needs at the school and three of them are mine!

A few families in the sample felt very cut off from the mainstream. They tended to be those with neither parent in work, with children who had constant care needs and who therefore found it very difficult to access ordinary facilities or to keep up ordinary networks. Despite feeling that they were doing a good job which was often rewarding, they were very conscious of the separateness and differentness of their lives. Furthermore, they could see no prospect of any change in their circumstances in the near or distant future and, as the children grew up, they expected their situation to become even more confined.

Networks and neighbours

Families without helpful relatives who lived nearby felt even more isolated. A few had supportive networks among friends, but friendships had often been hard for parents to maintain since having their disabled children. Some had developed new networks with other parents of disabled children and a few attended parent support groups, or had been instrumental in getting one set up in their area. Families seemed to benefit from attending groups related to particular conditions, particularly if this was backed up by a national organisation. They then felt that they had a lot in common with these other families. A few parents commented that having two disabled children had to some extent made them feel different from others in a parents' group. One parent also made the point that, despite the benefits that could be derived from meeting and talking things over with other parents:

> What you're actually doing is supporting each other. That's OK, but you can come home feeling three times as bad as when you went.

It is likely that families with more than one disabled child will be extra busy and have particular difficulty in finding sitters for both children in order to attend meetings. The South Asian parents who took part in the study were the least likely to be in touch with other parents except within the family. Either support networks did not exist locally or these mothers had difficulties in getting out. Some said they were too tired to do so like this parent, who said:

> I have not the time or the energy to make contact with other families in a similar position.

Several families who took part in the study had experienced hostility from neighbours. This was related to the behaviour of their children or the noise they made or resentment at the adaptations or benefits they seemed to enjoy, such as an extension to the house or an adapted vehicle. Such hostility added, of course, to the families' isolation. This was also true for some of the South Asian families in the study. Some had experienced racism and negative attitudes about their children from the wider community, whilst others felt there was general concern and understanding. Workers at a national helpline for parents run by Contact a Family report similar hostility experienced by families with two or more disabled children, irrespective of which ethnic group they came from.

Summary

This chapter has dwelt on the differences experienced and perceived by family members when two or more children have significant impairments. Lifestyles and choices for everyone are less spontaneous and flexible. They are unlikely to have contact with many other families with more than one disabled child, even though most of the practitioners who took part in the study were in touch with more than one, if not several, families in a similar position in the locality. Feelings of being different from other families are compounded by far fewer opportunities to work or socialise.

Neighbourly and friendly attitudes and acceptance within informal networks could enable families to feel part of the neighbourhood and community. However, with one or two exceptions, for the families in the sample, friends and neighbours played a minor role in terms of 'hands on' support to the family.

Together with consequent low incomes for families with severely disabled children, the extra care demands of at least two of the children can thus lead to severe social disadvantage and the possibility of social exclusion for all family members.

Practice points

It is vital to consider how families with two or more severely disabled children could be helped to lead more ordinary lives. Part of this is to recognise the likelihood that *all family members* will experience social exclusion, unless serious efforts are made to prevent this. Professionals and service providers have an important role to play, and might consider the following:

- How can parents be supported if they want to work?
- Are there things which would allow a freer lifestyle? e.g. pagers, mobile phones, answerphones, transport, taxis?
- Can care for the disabled children be arranged out of hours, so that other family members can pursue other interests and have a social life?
- Could networks between families with more than one disabled child be facilitated for those who wish to meet others in the same position?
- By working with other agencies, what leisure opportunities can be developed for disabled children, including those with complex needs, and how can they be helped to access them?

4   Managing day to day

This chapter will look in more detail at how the requirements for extra support and attention are managed *within* the family. It will identify the particular difficulties that arise for families in meeting their children's needs, which suggests the need for support from *outside* the family.

Tasks and time

It is well recognised that caring for a severely disabled family member takes up a considerable amount of time, whether this is directly helping a child or dealing with tasks generated by their impairments. Thus, these families are fitting more tasks into the same amount of time and often talk about needing more hours in the day. Domestic chores will obviously increase with the number of disabled children:

> The washing machine's on three times a day. It's never off, is it? It'll be back on in a minute. Yesterday, we had to do all the bedding for all the three children.

Some families managed by giving the housework low priority, especially during school holidays. A few families who could afford it employed someone to help clean or do the ironing. Only one family in the sample was currently getting any help from social services that included domestic tasks.

Caring tasks can vary, however, in how much time they take from day to day. For example, feeding a child who has difficulties in chewing and swallowing may take a long time but, if he or she is off colour, a meal might take two hours instead of one. Davies (1994) uses the concept of 'process time', rather than 'clock time', to describe how the needs of the care receivers determine how long a task will take. Parents or other carers frequently undertake several caring tasks at once, such as feeding one child while supervising another, who may run off, at the same time as having to talk to a social worker on the phone. It is evident that interruptions and waiting are inevitable in such scenarios.

This adds to the tension between 'process time' and 'clock time' and the problems for families when deadlines have to be met. A good example of this is seen at busy times of the day, such as early morning, when children need to be ready for school transport.

> Then I dress Kerry and Josh and you dress Darren, don't you, and see to him. And then I get the breakfasts ready, then Keith sits and feeds them while I'm getting the coats out, shoes out or whatever and bringing his buggy down. And making sure their bags are packed with the things they'll need for school. You know, one's doing one thing, whilst the other's doing another and then, when the bus pulls off, we have a coffee and say 'Morning'!

Families seem to manage these very busy times by having a clear routine and division of labour, often organised with military precision. These were the occasions when two carers were most needed, working as a team. At such times, if one was absent or unavailable, an extra pair of hands supplied by a service agency or another source could clearly be most helpful. Comments like 'It's a 24-hour job' or 'There's never enough time for everyone' were common.

Simultaneous demands

One of the particular issues for families with more than one severely disabled child is the need to meet the support needs of two or more very vulnerable children *at the same time*. This is, of course, an experience shared by any parent with two or three small children but, when the children have a severe disability, the nature and degree of support and care will be more extensive and continue well beyond infancy, often into adulthood.

In meeting and balancing the care needs of several children or young people at once, parents were also striving to give each child enough individual attention. This was understandably difficult when one demanded more attention then the other(s), particularly if the incompatibility or impairments of the children meant that some of their needs for companionship and care could not be met by each other:

Well, we felt to make Tony as independent as we could, we needed to spend the time with him, but Gary's nursing needs and his needs overall were increasing, so whenever Gary's here, I'm sort of with Gary.

Families frequently felt that they would have liked to have given more time to each child. One mother, whose older child needed a constant response and whose younger child had multiple impairments, said:

'Every night I promise my son I'll play with him the next day, but I never do.'

Some parents had concerns about the safety of the children because of the severity of their condition or their behaviour and a number needed constant surveillance. This meant that, at times, they would be trying to supervise children in different parts of the house. They were in separate rooms because they might be of risk to one another, or because they wanted privacy, or because their needs might best be met individually.

A few children without verbal skills were likely to resort to physical aggression when frustrated, because they were unable to argue. This then tended to aggravate the behaviour of the other children. Some families commented on the rivalry between children for parental attention. Others talked about their children sometimes defending each other and ganging up on their parents, which was hard to manage because of the children's limited understanding:

They were getting over the top with each other. Well, they had to be separated and when I was getting cross with Lucy, telling her to go to her room and calm down, Adam got very upset and he does, you see, and this makes it so difficult, because she will say, 'Go and tell mummy off, she shouldn't have said that to me!' and it's not just a game, he really means it, and he gets so upset by it. You think, well, how are we going to win at this one?

It is easy to see the benefits for such families in having individual time with children, either through one parent or carer doing something with each child in turn, or by a worker or volunteer occupying the other child or children. In a few situations where it was particularly difficult for parents to meet the complex needs of two or more disabled children, residential schooling had been considered or arranged. Although, on balance, this had helped all family members, parents suggested that if they had had only one disabled child, he or she would have remained at home.

There was a general concern among some parents that the presence of a severely disabled brother or sister in the family made life more difficult for another disabled child or young person. Also, because of the restrictions of the parents' time and energies, it reduced the prospects for each child's individual development. Comparing the long-term outcomes for disabled children from families with one or two affected children is beyond the scope of this study, but was a question raised by several parents and professionals who participated in the research.

At home

Disabled children spend much more of their time at home with their families than their non-disabled peers (Mulderij, 1996). Sometimes, the nature of a child's condition, such as severe epilepsy, means that someone must be with them at all times. Children may need equipment that is difficult to move about and requires sufficient storage space. Using equipment such as hoists and bathing aids, for instance, tends to take longer than parents lifting children manually (Oldman and Beresford, 1998). Therefore, care routines using equipment can actually use more time at home for parents and children. All these factors have a greater impact when there are two or more disabled children.

Furthermore, as they grow older, severely disabled children are much less likely to visit friends' houses, play outside or have access to inclusive leisure opportunities. This means that the natural breaks that parents and older children have from each other outside school never develop. It also emphasises the importance of a suitable environment at home.

A recent study (Oldman and Beresford, 1998) examined the suitability of housing for disabled children and their families. Three-quarters of those surveyed said their home was unsuitable in some way. Factors such as having stairs, no downstairs toilet, not enough space, an unsuitable garden and a difficult location were most frequently mentioned. As well as the importance of physical features, 'psychological space' was also found to be crucial. Families with children whose disability meant that the fabric and contents of the house were frequently damaged felt demoralised and without any sanctuary. All of these factors were identified in this study, too. Sometimes, parents felt compelled to manage situations by locking doors to certain rooms or making a room for the child or children which was padded, had strong glass and other features.

More commonly, and for several families in the sample, a home needed to be adapted to accommodate the physical requirements of the disabled children, for example, with ramps, lifts, accessible showers or special downstairs extensions. As well as being complicated and time-consuming to achieve with very limited public funding, these changes may mean that living space for the rest of the family is compromised, becomes dominated by the disability, and does not necessarily meet everyone's needs. In the following example, the adaptations did not meet the needs of *both* the disabled children:

> We needed the house adapted for both boys so, yes, we needed a through-floor lift. But it had to be one that was suitable for Gary and we had to move Tony's bedroom [which was made smaller by the lift]. Now they were gonna say, 'Oh, he can stay in the little room that he's in'. I said, 'You can't do that, he can't get his wheelchair in there'.

Therefore, disabled children can be very restricted in where they go, even at home. Those with physical disabilities may be limited to two or three rooms. Families frequently described their need for adequate space, including a garden which could accommodate special play equipment and privacy from neighbours.

> I would have told anybody with special needs children never to buy a semi-detached house. You need a place of your own; you need a big piece of land where you can let the kids enjoy themselves and play.

Going out as a family

As well as the limitations and frustrations at home, parents frequently described the practical difficulties and exhaustion involved in taking out two severely disabled children together. This is particularly the case if there is a lone parent or one parent is at work during the school holidays:

> But we just find like with having two of them, you know, like I find I'm stuck like. If one of them's poorly, you know, like just getting to shops and things.

Managing a visit to a supermarket may be restricting for the children as well:

> We just take them two out for the drive in the car, really, and I just go in the shop and do the shopping, and they just listen to the radio in the car.

This underlines the necessity for these families of having suitable transport. Having to use public transport or occasionally taxis could be impossible or very stressful for families and most would have preferred the privacy and flexibility of their own transport. Accessibility and acceptance at places to visit, such as new shopping centres, was potentially liberating and contrasted with the bad experiences of many families:

> As they get older, it's harder to be a normal family, because you can't go to a restaurant, you can't do the things you'd like to do. ... We took ours to the pictures once and they turned them away.

It is to be hoped that the gradual implementation of the Disability Discrimination Act (1996) should begin to ensure equal access, so that these children and their families are no longer made to feel second-class citizens.

Summary

It is apparent that bringing up all dependent children consumes a large amount of resources in terms of time, effort and space. If a child has an impairment, the amount of time spent supporting them will be far greater and over a longer period, and special consideration will need to be given to adapting the family home. When two or more children in a family have severe impairments, these issues are exacerbated and some new dimensions are created.

Pressure is increased on the time and energies of parents and other family members as they try to meet multiple needs simultaneously. The family home may become unsuited to the management of these extra responsibilities. All members of a family may feel that their lives are restricted physically and in terms of opportunities to do other things. Parents are under great pressure to be in the right place at the right time, according to the demands of their daily routine.

However, ameliorating factors are the compatibility and companionship of the children, having enough people around who can work as a team and parents feeling that they have adequate resources to care for the children as they would wish. The role of support agencies, then, is to understand the particular pressures on these families, their resources and managing strategies and to aim to minimise the problems and barriers that they face. Families' experience of support is the subject of the next chapter.

Practice points

This section has indicated some of the difficulties that families face when caring for two or more children who need a considerable amount of support. In particular, they are often short of help and time, especially at busy times of the day, or in relation to particular tasks or needs. There are many ways in which support agencies could help, through offering to all families those services that families with sufficient incomes tend to purchase for themselves:

- Providing help with the extra domestic work created, which frees families to have more time with their children.
- Targeting help at the most useful times, *as identified by families themselves*, can be an efficient use of limited resources.
- Offering extra pairs of hands that can substitute for one or two carer(s) is a valuable source of support if provided by familiar, trusted and flexible helpers.
- Providing adequate help in the school holidays and at weekends, when it may be impossible for one carer to cope safely alone and in a way that benefits the children.
- Setting up contingency plans for unexpected events and emergencies, such as the ill health of a parent or child.
- Helping families to plan how to make their home suitable for their needs, through adaptations or acquiring special equipment.

5 Families' experiences of outside support

> They have an emotional need, which is greater, obviously, with two rather than with one. Another big thing is that the actual physical need is tremendous. The actual caring; it's the practicalities that are increased. The other thing is the need for input from all areas, it should be smooth, they shouldn't have to fight for everything, but they have to. *And it's harder to battle for two than it is for one.*
>
> Community Nurse

It is apparent from the accounts in previous chapters that families with two or more severely disabled children can encounter extra difficulties associated with their double caring responsibilities. Whatever the rewards, most families and their individual members would like to have the opportunities to lead lives like other people. So how far does the support they receive enable this to happen?

In this chapter, families' experiences of outside support are explored with a view to inform current thinking about how such support might be improved. Again, a *whole-family approach* is central.

What's on offer

Traditionally, support to families with severely disabled children involved hospitalisation, often at some distance from home. Nowadays, nearly all disabled children live with their families. Community care policies and the development of attitudes that children with disabilities are 'children first' (Children Act, 1989) have led, in the past 20 years or so, to the development of different kinds of support to children and their families. Most health districts now have child development centres and teams, primarily for children below school age. These offer diagnosis and assessment of children leading to interventions or monitoring by specific therapists, which are overseen and reviewed by paediatricians and a multidisciplinary team. Once a child enters school, these therapies are more likely to be provided at school and, by now, local authority social services may also be offering support to the family. This usually aims to give disabled children more 'ordinary' experiences, and also to give their carers a break.

In the past decade, there has been a burgeoning of schemes providing short breaks for children with another 'link' family, as well as accommodation in hostel-type care, usually for a few children at a time. Projects providing care at home for short periods have also developed, as well as befriending schemes where a disabled child is linked with someone, perhaps a student, for leisure activities. Overall, however, such provision is in short supply and unevenly distributed between areas and populations (Chamba and others, 1999). For example, none of the South Asian families who took part in the study were receiving any support from social services.

Quality and quantity

Analysis of the accounts of all the families involved in the study indicates that families often seek more extensive help, in terms of both amount and scope, in order for their lives to become more like those of their peers. For instance, nearly all mothers said they would like to work, but none was receiving the level of support which would have made this possible. Flexibility of support, especially in short-term care, would also enable them to have a more spontaneous lifestyle and provide a more ready response at stressful times or in an emergency. Parents also wanted help that replicated the range and standards of care that they tried to provide themselves and offered suitable experiences that their children enjoyed. Otherwise, they expressed reluctance or unease at using a service in which they were not confident, especially in those few instances where children had been actually harmed while being accommodated away from home. In other words, in line with research findings about families with one disabled child, these families generally wanted more from services in terms of *quality* and *quantity* (Beresford, 1995).

Early support for families

Families may come to recognise that two or more of their children have severe disabilities at much the same or different times. Whenever or however this happened, parents described their devastation and bewilderment in the early days[1].

Exceptionally, parents felt overwhelmed by the number of professionals who called to see them at this time. However, only one or two families said they had had any emotional support in the early days, and then for only a brief period. Most described being 'left to get on with it on our own'. The support they tended to receive, if any, was of a practical nature and focused on the developmental needs of the child or children. Looking back, several families commented that in the early days, in a state of shock, they were poorly placed to know what kind of help they wanted from those they had only just met:

> It was nearly all practical. The social worker came round and she was always asking how was we. I think when you don't know people and that, anyway, you just say 'Oh, fine'. You know, it's a favourite line.

Almost all the parents who took part in the study considered that the early years had been the worst and that they would have benefited from more support:

> You learn to cope with them as they get older, but when they're younger, it's desperately hard. You wonder what you've been born, you know? You're teaching yourself. I think if we had more support in the home...

Perhaps one reason that families felt unsupported at this time was the limited resources available, as well as the number of different personnel that might be contacting parents about different aspects of a child's development. When there are so many other areas of concern, it appears that emotional support can often be overlooked. McConachie (1997) has suggested that parents are confronting a real psychological emergency in the early days, best addressed by the key worker model, where a single specialised professional can support the family on all fronts. Those families in the study who felt best supported did mention a particular professional, such as a health visitor, whom they had known prior to

[1] It is planned to publish a separate report based on material gathered from parents about this aspect of their experiences.

diagnosis and who could play a multi-faceted role both in accessing help and providing it herself.

Appointments

A paediatrician was often a key professional while parents were trying to obtain a diagnosis for their children. Most families who took part in the study continued to see a paediatrician once or twice a year. This focused on the individual child's condition and they were sometimes referred for further treatment or consultation. For example, some families were still undergoing genetic investigations, or children might require surgery to fit a gastrostomy as they got older and feeding became more difficult. These consultations often now took place at the children's special school. Families found this much more convenient than taking the children, either together or separately, to hospital appointments.

> Now he goes to the school, so we book it in the school. And then what they do, the kids are in the classroom, we go and find them, and they just bring them up and then take them back to the classroom.

Families appreciated this continuing if nominal contact with someone who knew the children well, although the medical role diminished if children did not have continuing physical problems. A few families also attended regional clinics for children with a particular medical condition and welcomed the expertise and coordination they encountered there: 'We go to the regional centre for a day every eight weeks and everything is seen to there'.

However, many families were still required to attend numerous appointments to see other health professionals in relation to one or other of their children, often on different days at the same or a different hospital. This was time-consuming, disruptive of routine, tiring and stressful.

> Well, you see, you tend to be at the mercy of these people, because they say 'Right, come to the hospital that day and you'll go to the ENT place that day and you'll go somewhere else that day' and they don't think you've got a life. They just think you're there to sit in their waiting room.

One parent suggested the cross-referencing of children on hospital computers, so that their visits could be better planned.

Other situations could require parents to be in two places at once, for example, school transport. Disabled children may attend different schools from each other and their siblings, all getting to and from school by different means. When her son changed schools, this mother had to negotiate that both children were picked up from home, rather than meeting one at the end of the road: 'In theory, it might have worked but if one of the children was poorly or at home and I had to drag them to the pick-up point...'

Help at home

There were two types of help at home that had been experienced by some families in the sample: help with domestic tasks from a home help and help with looking after the children provided by a voluntary agency. Usually, both involved unqualified staff; only one family had been offered nursing help at home.

Typically, this support was for two or four hours a week. One family received eight hours' help, but they acknowledged that this was unusual. In this case, four hours was on a Friday evening to enable the parents to go out for the evening. The other four hours were split into three sessions of one hour 20 minutes to cover the feeding and bathing of one child. This was targeted to cover one of the busiest times of the day and with the child who needed most physical care, and was appreciated by her 18-year-old brother who could therefore have some time to himself when he came home from work:

> It's not so bad when I come home from work, 'cos like Sally's [care worker] here a lot and that takes summat off me, you know what I mean. I can go and sit down for half an hour, but when I come home and Sally's not here and Paul's [stepfather] not here, I give my mum a hand. My mum can't lift her, Joanne weighs more than my mum.

Fitting in

However, the potential conflict between 'process time' and 'clock time' (Davies, 1994) suggests that sometimes caring tasks may have to be rushed, rather than going at the child's pace, to fit in with the agency's timetable. It also highlights the very small amounts of time generally being offered to families, if they receive the service at all. One lone mother, for example, suggested that 16 hours a week would be a reasonable amount of support during the school holidays:

> But if you could think to yourself, well, this girl comes on a Tuesday morning, 'Right, we'll go swimming'. Because with a lot of these children, especially when you've got two with special needs, you need two adults. You can't do it with one adult and two children, you just can't do it. Or if you knew she was coming, you could say, 'Right, well, see if you can play a game with them or something and I'll get on with the ironing', and you could sort of plan.

Families are busiest before and after school and at weekends, but support is less likely to be available at unsocial hours. Many disabled children have sleeping difficulties, rendering their parents permanently tired. However, only one lone parent, met during the study, was receiving help overnight to encourage a better sleep pattern in one of her children. Another parent who has two children who sleep poorly pointed to this gap in support:

> I don't think this is something they'd ever do because of the finance of it, but to be able to call someone and say, 'I've had a bad night, will you come round for an hour while I just get my head down?'

Other factors affecting the usefulness of practical help at home seem to be the continuity of carer, the attitudes of those providing the help and the degree of intrusion into family life. Families preferred the same carer with whom they had built up trust over a period, someone who slotted into their way of doing things, was uncritical and flexible. If these features were not present, families might prefer to do without such help. The following quotes illustrate some of these issues:

> Every couple of months we had a new home help. I know it sounds weird, but then you like had to train them.

> The point is, if you've been doing it yourself and you've been balancing one on one hand and one on the other you just get used to it and if somebody else comes in, it takes twice as long to explain to them.

> Some of them couldn't do enough for you. They'd bend over backwards. Others did as little as possible. You know, they didn't fit in with you. You had to fit in with them.

These difficulties could make families feel undermined and intruded upon, despite desperately needing such help. They are well used to visits from various professionals, such as health visitors, the GP and social workers to the family home but these calls generally involve talking and information giving. Workers who get involved practically in domestic and caring tasks, if badly managed, can seem to cross public/private boundaries in a way that is difficult for families to control. Consequently, some families choose to employ someone to clean the house or do the ironing if they have sufficient resources; they are then more in charge of the arrangements.

A complete break

The majority of families used, or would like to have used, short-term care for their children, especially if this was not available within the extended family. Particularly important for parents was the need for times when they had a break from both children. However briefly, this could offer families the chance to relinquish their caring role and do other things.

For those in the study, however, it was unusual for this to be available unless the children had similar impairments and were close in age. Only two families in the sample whose children had the same disabilities were currently receiving short-term care in the same establishment at the same time. Two brothers with the same condition from another family were being introduced to a 'link' family with a view to them visiting simultaneously.

Generally, the system offered care away from home which parents had come to use once they felt their children were ready to stay overnight. Some children had a 'link' family they visited every few weeks for day care or an overnight stay. More children had short-term care in a residential hostel on a regular pattern of care, usually one weekend a month. In these ways, they were offered the same support for individual children as families with one disabled child.

If the children were different in terms of their disabilities or more than a year or two apart in age, another family was unlikely to feel they could manage their needs together. Residential units, too, usually group children attending at the same time in terms of age and type of disability. So, in order to give the rest of the family a break, support agencies would have to arrange care for different children at different settings and try to ensure that schedules of care on offer, usually on a monthly cycle, sometimes coincided. If this could not be arranged, or perhaps one child was not receiving respite care at present, families felt that they never had a complete rest. 'We can't get all the three children away from us, so we're not getting that break'.

Usually, however, there was no choice about whether children had short breaks with their sibling(s) at the same or different times, even if they were staying at the same establishment. Neither was there a choice about whether this would be provided in a residential or family setting. Parents felt, and professionals often acknowledged, that children tended to be fitted into what was available: 'Instead of thinking about it, they just use like a number ... "She'll be alright there, he'll be alright there, that'll be fine"'.

However, some families may also feel that it is important that the children have a break from each other: 'We try and make sure that Tony's not there when Gary's there, 'cos it defeats the object otherwise'.

The lack of preferred support is likely to be particularly felt if a service has been reduced or the criteria changed:

> It were beautiful then, everything worked out lovely, we could go out for the night together, but now we've got our Becky at home or Robbie at home, one's away, one's back at home, so you're only getting half a break.

One family had managed to arrange care in their own home while they went away for a week twice a year. They considered that this was the most suitable arrangement for their four disabled teenagers and one adult, rather than them being accommodated in separate establishments. However, this had been difficult to achieve and had required the advocacy of a voluntary sector worker and the support of a new social worker. Especially with the difficulties in recruiting families to care for children and young people with complex disabilities (Shared Care UK, 1997), such an arrangement where carers take over from parents and siblings in the family home would offer another option that would suit some children and their parents.

Variability in short breaks

Some families in the study had not been able to access short-term care for one or more of their children. Families whose children were in mainstream school tended to be offered only a limited service, with short-term care targeted on more severely disabled children. Others were either on a waiting list for a suitable family or their child's requirements were such that they did not fit the available provision. In one area, for instance, residential respite was only available to children with nursing needs. In a neighbouring area, this was only available to children without nursing needs. Similarly, in another district, the family of a child with a terminal illness found it difficult to access any home nursing, whereas in another area there was a community nursing team who were able to provide nursing support to relieve families towards the end of a child's life.

Families whose children had a terminal condition did have contact with the regional children's hospice, although demand for its service meant that they only used the hospice about twice a year. They liked the high standard of care provided which included the whole family, with family members given the choice about how much to be with the children during their stay. The positive attitude of the staff was contrasted with that of the local respite facility by one mother:

> But as I said, nothing fazes them. We went to pick 'em up and 'Oh they've been lovely, Kerry's been lovely.' But she hadn't, I mean, she's full of it, she'll tire 'em out. But you go and pick 'em up from The Beeches and it's 'Oh, she's been a bugger, oh, she's been up to everything'. Well, you think like, she hasn't, she's just been her normal self.

None of the South Asian families involved in the study were accessing short-term care. Overall, they felt that the provision on offer was culturally inappropriate, that the language and customs of the children would not be understood. Parents would have preferred day care and support at home from someone who could play with the children for a few hours, rather than overnight respite, as expressed by this mother:

> Instead of having respite care, I think that some sort of day care system would be very good. ... I would prefer single-sexed services because of our culture and the way we have been brought up.

Some professionals interviewed also suggested that putting more scarce resources into carers going into the home, rather than overnight respite, would be more cost-effective and therefore provide a service to more families. However, often such support was not well developed locally, and then families encountered long waiting lists and delays, mostly receiving no practical support with either child. It would appear, then, that those families who have greatest difficulties in managing, because of the children's characteristics or the incompatibilities between them, are least likely to be getting the kind of support they prefer. In any case, families generally wanted a range of provision to meet a range of needs rather than an either/or option.

Children's views

Short-term breaks are generally designed to give families a break from caring, but also offer the disabled children enjoyable experiences. It was also very important to families that children appeared to be happy and safe when they were using these services. However, it was unusual for children to be consulted by professionals about the services they used. Although few were able to express a verbal opinion, one 14-year-old said one of his favourite things was going on residentials with his school. Another boy had been able to tell his mother that he did not like the respite centre he and his brother attended. She no longer sent them there but, as there was no alternative service available, they now did not have any short breaks.

Disabled and non-disabled children who were able to speak, talked enthusiastically about any hobbies, interests and social activities, however limited, and were pleased to be doing the same sorts of things as other kids. They and their parents would have liked more such opportunities to be available to them locally. Some of the more severely disabled children had no such outlets and usually only went out to go to school or to short-term care or on brief outings with their parents.

Leisure opportunities

Some families in the overall sample did access the kind of day-time support that the South Asian mothers had in mind, for one or more of their children. Playschemes for disabled children, often available for a week or two of the summer holidays and usually organised in the voluntary sector, were popular with families. However, sometimes parents of children with complex needs worried whether young volunteers would be able to cope and their children would be safe.

Despite a range of impairments, none of the children in the sample attended schemes that were integrated with non-disabled peers. Nevertheless, day leisure activities are seen as normative opportunities for children and young people, which are particularly helpful to families if children are accommodated together: 'We were lucky because they picked the same week for both children, because I'd got terrible visions of one going one week and one the next'.

Just a few children in the sample accessed after-school provision for a few hours a week or a fortnight. One went to an after-school club at a respite centre and, in another area, an 'outreach' scheme collected children from home in groups of two or three and took them off for an enjoyable activity and a meal. Three children in the sample used this service. One parent described how this provided some timely leisure opportunities for her son, thus leaving her time with her other child:

> I put him on the minibus, give him a five-pound note and they take him out. ... Helen doesn't arrive home till after he's gone, which then gives me a few minutes to sort myself out and then give Helen my attention, and by the time he comes in it's sort of 'Get undressed, in the bath, have your supper, off to bed!'

Such projects offer the chance for children to meet and make friends and see other children outside school, an opportunity also provided by residential short-term care.

Some teenagers attended special clubs in the evenings or at weekends, sometimes with their brother(s) or sister(s). This often required parents to transport them to and fro, especially in rural areas. If transport was provided, this made young people feel more independent and freed up their parents' time.

Just one or two families had carers or befrienders coming into the home to play with children or take them out for a few hours and several were, or had been, involved in sitting schemes to enable parents to go out in the evening. For those without access to such support, finding sitters was very difficult, especially if family members were not available.

Family resources

Most of the families in the sample were reliant on benefits. In those families where one partner was in employment, families were also concerned about money, because of the extra costs of disability generally and specific expenditure such as housing adaptations or special equipment that they frequently needed. Recent research has highlighted the extra costs of bringing up a severely disabled child. This is estimated to be three times that of a child without disability (Dobson and Middleton, 1998). Having two or more severely disabled children is likely to add to these extra costs and, for the parents in this study, there was no prospect of a change in their financial circumstances in the foreseeable future.

Several families had experienced problems with claiming appropriate benefits and some pointed to what they considered to be anomalies in the system. A few benefits, such as child benefit and the disabled child premium, could be claimed for each child. Disability Living Allowance is a benefit that also considers the individual child's impairments and needs for support and awards corresponding bands of benefit. However, these families are caring for more than one disabled child, and therefore the demands they make on their families' energies will be *cumulative*. For example, two children may each need attention at night two or three times a week. Therefore, their parent(s) could be disturbed almost every night of the week. However, each individual child will be assessed as warranting benefit at the lower or middle rate rather than the higher rate. Parents suggested that a whole-family approach by the benefits system might afford a truer reflection of their doubled caring responsibilities and costs.

Where neither parent was working, both parents were able to claim Invalid Care Allowance, one for each child. However, even working part time could put a parent above the earning threshold for this benefit. Lone parents were only able to claim in relation to one of their children, even though having more than one disabled child made them much less likely to be able to work than a lone parent with one disabled child.

As children reached adulthood and left school, some benefits changed and some were paid directly to the young person themselves. However, this money was frequently regarded as essential to the family as a whole, and difficulties could arise if they were then charged substantially for services. Natural and adoptive parents could feel penalised for caring for their children over the years and expressed the opinion that their children's care would be much more expensive, but of inferior quality, if they could no longer cope. Yet they were still struggling financially:

I mean, a lot of parents continue to care for their disabled child when they're no longer a child, when they're an adult. And there should be a proper recognition: why can't they be paid the same as if they went to an adult placement in another house?

Most of the families in the sample had been helped in some way by the Family Fund Trust. This help was offered in kind, for example, washing machines, dryers and payment for driving lessons. This was much appreciated, as was the willingness to help of the visitors who had followed up the claim that either the parents or a professional had made on their behalf. Many parents had also been awarded the cost of a holiday in the UK. However, several families pointed out the extra costs and difficulties of taking two disabled children away from home. Sometimes, this involved taking an extra adult along, too. Some families found it easier to have separate holidays with different children. It was suggested that the extra requirements of these families should be considered when making a grant for a family holiday.

Aids and adaptations

As described in Chapter 4, families who took part in the study were frequently bringing up their children in homes that were less than ideal. A number had had their homes adapted in some way, but sometimes addressing one situation only partially solved the problem or indeed created other difficulties. With two or more severely disabled children, it was particularly difficult to ensure that any changes to the home suited the needs of both children, as well as the rest of the family, and were also culturally appropriate. Here, one parent mentions the continuing difficulties, despite an extension to her home:

> We had the extra bedroom built downstairs, but I still have Syed [age 12] upstairs with us, because I don't like him to be downstairs on his own at night. This means that I have to carry him upstairs and this is very difficult for me to do with my varicose veins but I have no choice, it is either that or sleeping downstairs with Syed, which I cannot do because Jameed gets up in the night as well.

However, two families in the sample had moved within public housing to homes that had been specially adapted overall to meet the particular families' requirements. Both talked about the benefits to the family and reduction of stress since moving

house. In one case, the involvement of a worker from a
support organisation relating to a particular condition had
helped the family and the housing authority to think about
the family's future as well as present needs. This suggests
that addressing the families' needs overall, which may
necessitate moving house, is more successful and probably
more cost-effective than looking at housing problems piece-
meal and in the short term.

Those families living in their own homes, with a parent in
employment, were less likely to have achieved the changes
they needed. They had been expected to make a sizeable
contribution to the cost, which they did not think they could
afford, and the whole assessment process had taken a
considerable time. One such family was still having to carry
severely disabled teenagers upstairs, because of a stalemate
with the appropriate authorities. Whatever the details of such
negotiations, these young people's needs were not being met.

As with families with one disabled child, delays were
common in getting equipment, such as special seating for
children. Sometimes, they had been made to feel they were an
expensive family because they needed two of everything, and
it had been suggested to more than one family that children
could share equipment which they might need at the same
time, such as when eating. By contrast, parents expressed the
view that they were a providing a cost-effective service, but
this should not be regarded as 'two for the price of one'!

Summary

Many of the elements of the support they were receiving
found favour with families. Most of their criticisms and
suggestions for improvements were often to do with small
changes in arrangements to make care better coordinated and
better timed to suit pressure points in family life. Similarly,
they wanted services to be more suitable for individual
children, as well as sensitive to their particular family
situation so that *everyone's needs* would be better met.
Frequently, they felt that the services on offer were all right
in themselves but that too little help was available. When it
was offered, it tended to be inflexible and bound by bureau-
cratic rules. From the experiences of the South Asian families
who took part in the study who were receiving very little or no
help, it would seem that there is a danger that families from

minority ethnic groups are not receiving the support they need, and that services need to be made both more accessible and culturally appropriate.

Practice points

Generally, families like to have:

- the needs and views of all children considered;
- dovetailed appointments with doctors, hospitals and therapists;
- a complete break at times, outside school hours;
- support that allows individual time with each child;
- services that fit in with their family and cultural situation;
- short breaks that the children enjoy and in which parents have confidence;
- flexibility and choice in short-break arrangements, including day care and carers coming to the home to help;
- accessible and supported leisure opportunities for the disabled children, especially in school holidays;
- prompt and efficient access to suitable aids and equipment;
- home adaptations that make life easier for the whole family and are easy to manage;
- an adequate income and other resources so that money is not a major concern;
- experienced key professionals who work with all family members and across agencies;
- meetings which consider each individual child and the whole-family situation.

These last two points show the importance families attach to receiving a streamlined, 'seamless' service. The detail of delivering such support is looked at in the next chapter.

6 Coordinating and delivering suitable services

This chapter will consider some aspects of the delivery and organisation of services which seem most relevant to the provision of the coordinated support that families with two or more severely disabled children require. The number of different agencies and professionals that families with a disabled child might be in touch with has frequently been noted (Beresford, 1995). This is likely to be increased for families with more than one disabled child, especially if children have different conditions, attend different schools and so on. Although professional input was appreciated, parents in the study could feel overwhelmed. Thus, coordination in terms of time and place and between personnel and agencies is vital, though notoriously difficult to achieve (Audit Commission, 1994).

A key professional

It is well understood that families want a key person to help arrange and oversee the support they receive (Sloper and Turner, 1992; Beresford, 1995). However, analysis of material from the '1000 families' study (Lawton, 1998) indicated that families with two or more disabled children were slightly less likely to have a key worker than families with one child. The figures are 16 per cent compared to 22 per cent.

Families taking part in this study were asked to suggest a main professional who could be interviewed. Clearly, a number thought the person they nominated was their key worker, although the person concerned sometimes did not see themselves in this role. In reality, they were the first person a family would turn to if they wanted help. However, the professional, whether a social worker, community nurse or health visitor, often did not feel they had the remit to negotiate within and across agencies on their behalf. If they were then unable to provide what the family required, this could lead to disappointment and confusion.

Whatever their title or job description, families wanted someone who could take an overview of the family and develop a package of appropriate services. They praised workers who acted in this way: 'She goes in to assess families and assess the person that needs the help and builds up a package and a programme and puts it all in and sorts it all out'.

Parents also appreciated someone who understood what the family required and were active in finding solutions:

> She was listening and she was doing. She listened in an alert frame of mind, with her mind grappling with the problem, and her mind focused on us. And she'd phone and give me updates and come up and see us. I mean, she kept us informed of what she was doing. So that we didn't think, 'Oh heck, I wonder if she's just a load of old talk'. You know, she was really good.

It was also helpful if any professional the family encountered, such as a GP or teacher, understood the situation of the whole family:

> It's nice to have someone who has an overall view. The doctor that we have in the practice now, he's the one who saw our need when we went for something else. And he sees us as a whole family. You know, not just as isolated people, but he sees the whole family need. And it's unusual.

Without such professionals who had a holistic view of the issues that concerned the family, these families found they had to compartmentalise their concerns. Feeling that someone really understood their children, their situation and their ways of managing things was clearly important to them. This was particularly true of the South Asian families who were usually dealing with workers who did not speak their first language and were not of the same ethnic origin:

> Only professionals that visit on a regular basis can understand the family's situation. There are three main things they don't understand – our religion, our culture and our way of life. ... The most difficult thing has been to make services clear about our needs.

All things to all people?

Despite professionals understanding the benefits of a whole-family approach and a key worker, this was often hard to achieve in practice. As a child approached adulthood, a transitional or adult services social worker became involved, so that the family would then have two workers for their children because of the difference in their ages. For one family, both the child and adult social workers tried to minimise problems that might arise by visiting the family at the same time. However, different teams within the same department are likely to have different budgets, thus complicating the streamlining of support.

Furthermore, it could be argued that it is preferable to have one worker per child to clarify the agency's role. This sometimes happened to help emphasise the individuality of children, such as when two community nurses worked in relation to different children in a family. This was evidently supportive for the workers concerned, who could discuss their approaches with a colleague. In relation to working with families with two disabled children more generally, one social worker did raise the issue of staff support and supervision, suggesting that such work was likely to be more stressful. As one community nurse commented: 'As I see it, some of these families manage on perpetual crisis level'.

The point was also made that, in supporting a family with complex needs, it is difficult for one worker to cover several roles and be an expert in all aspects of the family's difficulties. This might include, for instance, the management of epilepsy, benefits, arranging short breaks organised by another agency and the provision of aids and equipment, as well as providing emotional support to all family members. Sometimes, workers with large caseloads are trying to organise numerous aspects of a family's support almost single-handed. One suggestion was the prioritising of support for families with more than one severely disabled child, within protected caseloads.

Particularly in rural areas, where services are widely spaced, professionals have to be inventive in order to help families access the support they might need. Consequently, some were skilful in using local networks to create support for families away from the standard provision in urban areas, although this necessitated imagination and persistence:

> We haven't anything on tap and I think a lot of people find it quite challenging that they have to travel wherever they want any help from. They have to get in a car and go and quite a lot of them can't drive. . . . I try and match up all the services that go together, and see if we can get some help that way. . . . and try and match people

up with each other as well. ... You have got to scrounge around because they're not readily available, you have to find out where they are ... you have to go looking and get pushing, you have to push for services.

Support agencies now try to target their help in an accountable and cost-effective way. Input with a particular family may have to be justified in relation to the developmental needs of a particular child. Thus, a professional may become involved with a family as a worker from a specialised project, for children with a short-life expectancy, autism or challenging behaviour, for instance. This was the case for a few families in the sample. While such help can focus on the particular difficulties of individual children, these professionals can feel frustrated that they do not officially have a role in relation to other disabled children in the family or, indeed, to the family as a whole, as expressed by this social worker who had worked on such a scheme:

> I try to see myself working with the whole family in order to sort of try and understand their dynamics and try and get to know the boys a bit, but in truth most of the work was supporting Tricia and Gary. ... Personally, you know, I felt that it was in some ways a backward step that you had to fit people more into categories and couldn't be as flexible.

In one children's centre, health, social service and voluntary sector agency teams were housed in the same building, and there was an ethos of close collaboration. Here, it was suggested that families could contact any of the available professionals who worked with them. They in turn could pass a message to their colleague or discuss a problem on their behalf:

> If I like go to see a parent and they've been to see a paediatrician and they were unhappy about something. Or they want to discuss something. I can actually go and speak to that person face to face. Where I worked before, you were forever on the telephone trying to get hold of somebody. But I hope that's what it's like for parents, that they can ring one kind of door really, they will get a response from somebody.

A recent Social Services Inspectorate inspection (SSI, 1998) found that good collaborative practice was more likely to occur in multidisciplinary and, presumably, multi-agency centres. Where teams and agencies are separated by role, geography, or ethos, it is easier to blame each other for families receiving inadequate support.

Meetings and reviews

The difficulties of coordination within and between agencies were also manifest in the mechanisms that were available for reviewing packages of care.

For a few families in the sample, this happened at the same time and place for both children. This enabled the family's overall needs to be considered and avoid duplication. However, more frequently, review meetings were held to monitor use of a particular service, such as when children were accommodated overnight for short breaks or professionals met with parents to discuss the children's educational or developmental progress. Sometimes, social services or health staff attended a school review, but it was unusual to find procedures in place to consider all aspects of the children's and family's situation at the same time:

> Something that does need looking at is actually organising multidisciplinary meetings for these families, because it's all so time consuming. . . . I mean, I do communicate constantly, I spend hours on the phone. But we need something central to each, so we know where we're all going.

Professionals pointed out that meetings could become very large and time-consuming, if all those working with a family attended. One suggestion was for a key person from each agency who could then coordinate input from their colleagues. The observation was also made that meetings could sometimes be a substitute for providing services, which a family needed but were currently unavailable. Underlying this is the idea that discussion was better than nothing. While families wanted real opportunities to communicate their support needs and get their views across, they too did not want to attend 'talking shops', where nothing was decided.

Such meetings which were multi-agency generally involved specialist child disability services. However, in the experience of the families in the sample, some agencies and personnel which might be as important to families such as GPs and primary care teams, housing officials, transport and youth services were not included in meetings. This could then mean that crucial issues were not addressed and important loose ends were left untied.

Families then tended to feel that their total situation and how the different services impacted on each other were not being acknowledged. It was also more difficult for gaps between services to be recognised. Sometimes, parents did not know who should take the initiative in reviewing and accessing services, but had often done so themselves:

> I often wonder if and why it's not reviewed on a more regular basis. Maybe it's just a breakdown of communications or maybe it needs us to say. ... I've got quite alert now and I sort of phone people up and I say, 'Look, I want you to look at this'. ... I think we're well covered now, but only because we know how to tap into all the different services.

Parents of disabled children generally describe how they have to fight for appropriate support, and this was equally true of those families with two or more severely disabled children. This was time-consuming and stressful, and made parents particularly appreciative of the help of key professionals who were 'on the ball' when support was forthcoming, whether from a statutory or voluntary agency.

Flexibility

All the services described above that families were receiving were organised on a timetable usually planned well in advance. As has been noted, sometimes this was essential so that children could have short breaks that coincided. However, the downside of this was that services could rarely be flexible so that families could act spontaneously and, for instance, accept a last-minute invitation or, more crucially, be able to respond to an emergency. It was not unusual for families to have regular crises related to the health or behaviour of one or more of the children. This was twice as likely to happen with two or more severely disabled children. Equally, a parental illness was just as much of an emergency, when there were two very dependent children to care for.

In the quantitative study (Lawton, 1998), 21 per cent of the parents who had two disabled children said they had no-one to turn to if they were unwell, compared to ten per cent of parents of one disabled child. However, it was very unusual for contingency plans to be in place should such situations arise; only one family in the sample had a list of people who could come to the house at short notice if one of their children had to be hospitalised. Sometimes, an emergency bed for a child might be available, but as this parent pointed out: 'But because there's two of them, there's always one spare bed, but there's never two spare beds'.

Particularly for those families without flexible support from the extended family, how they would cope in an emergency and what would happen to the children was a big cause of worry. In order to plan for emergencies and offer some flexibility to these families, it therefore seems essential that enough spare capacity is built into provision rather than, once more, expecting families to fit in with services (SSI, 1998).

Services were generally organised on the assumption that each family would have one disabled child. Getting the right support to families with two or three severely disabled children is bound to be more complicated. Several professionals expressed frustration that the systems within which they worked do not allow them to be as flexible and creative for these families as they would have wished, such as in the example of carers coming to the family home so that parents could go away on holiday. It was then up to the doggedness of the workers and family involved to make services fit families.

Policy and practice points

Families support a *key worker system* to organise and oversee services for them. How can it be ensured that:

- He/she can work effectively across agencies? A key person in each main agency might be an alternative for some families.
- They have sufficient time and other resources to carry out their role creatively?
- Suitable supervision and support is in place for them in a potentially stressful and multifaceted role?
- A bilingual key worker is available to families for whom English is not their first language?

Reviews and meetings are costly and time-consuming for everyone involved. Can they be made to work effectively for families by:

- Allowing the needs and views of everyone in the family to be expressed?
- Considering alternatives that might be preferable to the family overall, rather than just reviewing a current service?

- Setting up mechanisms to involve personnel/agencies who do not attend meetings?
- Having opportunities to discuss the impact of the disabled children/young people, and their packages of care, on each other?
- Ensuring that all relevant aspects of a family's situation are discussed and that gaps in support are identified?
- Discussing ways in which collaboration can be achieved and improved?

Families have indicated that a system that was *flexible* enough to respond to changes of routine, individual preferences and emergencies would be especially supportive. Could this be achieved by, for example:

- more support at unsocial hours;
- responsive sitting arrangements for one or more children;
- explicit plans for emergencies drawn up with the family;
- two emergency beds rather than one;
- budgets and systems that could allow for creative packages of care?

7 Key messages and recommendations

This project has attempted to increase awareness and understanding of the particular circumstances of families with two or more severely disabled children and to examine their consequent support needs and how these might best be met. The implications for relationships within the family, changes in expectations and lifestyles, and individual and family identities have been described, drawing on the accounts of those who took part in the study and observations of family times. The day-to-day management of the extra tasks involved in the disabled children's care and support has been explored and, from the accounts of family members and key professionals, their positive and negative experiences of support services.

This final section summarises the principal issues from the report by highlighting, first, what service providers need to know about families with two or more severely disabled children and, second, how they might respond more effectively to their particular support needs.

What is important about families with two or more severely disabled children?

- The extra support needs of at least two disabled children affect *all family relationships*. Pressure on partnerships is created by the need for two carers. Siblings may be providing significant help, although reciprocity and companionship can also be important between the disabled children. Some grandparents and relatives provide considerable support, whilst negative reactions from others undermine the family. Informal networks outside the family are frequently reduced.
- *Families value each of their offspring* and want others, including professionals, to do so, too. Parents see them

foremost as individual children, whatever their impairments. They describe the rewards brought by their disabled children and some parents have created a family with two or more disabled children through family placement.

- Because the care needs of two or more severely disabled children frequently require two carers, in around half of these families neither parent is working. *Low incomes and caring lead to isolation and restricted lifestyles.* Parents would like to work and have an identity apart from parenting, perhaps using skills acquired through caring. Despite often feeling they are doing a good job, increased public visibility and scrutiny with more than one disabled child can be undermining and exaggerate feelings of being different.

- *Managing simultaneous demands is a key issue* for these families, as is giving each child individual attention. Domestic chores are increased, complicated by interruptions, and unexpected events are increasingly likely with two disabled children. A suitable home environment, two carers, transport and other resources all help.

- *Families prefer the service support they receive to be negotiated through one or two trusted key professionals* who understand the whole family situation and their overall needs. *They would like services to be coordinated*, for example, appointments, and timed to suit their routines. They find it important that all the professionals they have dealings with *communicate* with them and their children and with each other.

- *A complete break from caring plus individual time with their children* is what most parents want, but find hard to access. More support at busy times and during leisure activities for children would make life easier, as would the knowledge that support is flexible enough to accommodate family events and emergencies.

Improving support to families with two or more severely disabled children

Many of the needs of families and their requirements from support services are similar to those of families with one disabled child, though they are likely to need much more support. The *cumulative and complicating effects of caring for two or more children with extra support needs* means that services need to be sensitive to issues which are particular to them. Generally, support has been organised and offered on the assumption that families will have only one disabled child.

Because the specific situation of these families has not usually been recognised, support agencies will need to rethink, expand and develop their approaches when trying to support them. They will also need to consider how what these families require can be adequately resourced. Delivering services to these families is bound to be much more complex, so that managers and practitioners need to use the legislative framework and opportunities within government policy initiatives to work together at local level in order to provide families with the help that makes most sense to them.

The following points are a summary of the key issues for professionals to consider in their practice and planning in relation to families with two or more severely disabled children. For further suggestions, please refer to the 'practice points' at the end of each chapter.

- Services need to recognise that the *whole family*, fathers, siblings and grandparents, as well as mothers, are very often involved in caring, when there are two disabled children. These family members should be acknowledged and supported, too, and all individual perspectives and needs considered, while working with the family as a unit. The mutual benefits and problems of relationships between the disabled children are an important part of family dynamics. Services which can take account of the complexity of family life and relationships when arranging and reviewing packages of care will be the most effective.

- *Positive professional attitudes towards the disabled children* are important to families. In their early distress and in their continuing contact with services, they find workers who are sympathetic, informative, who listen to them and are non-judgmental to be supportive. It is also essential that workers outside specialised provision, in the health service, education or working to support families more generally are knowledgeable about childhood disability (DoH, 1999).

- Support systems which offer a *single-door coordinated approach* from the time of initial concerns are ideal, but often not in place. This coordination is especially crucial for families with two or more disabled children who might be dealing with large numbers of different professionals across a number of agencies. Otherwise, they could receive unrelated advice or pieces of support for different children which detract from their usefulness.

- Because of the cumulative effects of caring for two or more severely disabled children, these families are likely to need *more support*. It is also essential that what is provided is available when families are busiest, and *flexible* enough to respond to both family routines and emergencies, which are doubly likely with two disabled children.

- Agencies need to find ways to meet families' needs for more *freedom and choice*, through providing evening and weekend care, leisure opportunities for everyone in the family and accessible transport. Although such support is often given low priority, it would enable parents and children to feel less excluded, have lifestyles that are less restricted and experiences that most families take for granted.

- The opportunity to *juggle working and bringing up their children* would lessen isolation and enable families to feel more part of the mainstream, and often make them better off. The experience of parents who do manage to work suggests that this would require not only flexible employment and benefits structures, but also readily available and increased childcare and help at home. Equally, those who are unable or choose not to work should have the *cumulative costs* of their situation recognised by the benefits system.

Appendix   Research aims and methods

The overall objective of the research project was to raise awareness of the particular situation and support needs of families with two or more severely disabled children. In order to do this, there were three main aims:

- To estimate the numbers of such families in the UK, describe their characteristics and draw comparisons with families with one disabled child.
- To develop an understanding of their particular experiences and support needs related to caring for their disabled children.
- To identify forms of support appropriate to these families and make practice and policy suggestions.

The first part of the project met the first of these aims. Information about 100,000 families from the Family Fund Trust database was analysed to see how many had two or more disabled children. The disabling conditions of the children, and their severity, were investigated as far as possible and the circumstances of families compared with those of families with one disabled child, on a number of counts, such as family structure, family income, housing tenure and so on. Thirty-nine questionnaires from families with two disabled children from a previous study (Beresford, 1995) that had not been analysed also provided comparative material to complement the findings of the data from the database analysis (Lawton, 1998).

The work reported on in this project was designed to meet the other aims of the research by providing detailed accounts from families of bringing up two or more severely disabled children and their experiences of support services. Research methods were devised and piloted in order to include all immediate family members in the research, as well as a key professional nominated by each family.

Families were generally visited on three occasions. The first meeting was usually with parents alone to explain the purpose of the project and to interview them about their children and the family's circumstances, using a topic guide. Agreement was reached with parents to meet the children of the family on a subsequent visit and advice sought on how this meeting might best suit them. If possible, children and young people were written to or telephoned to make an arrangement with them directly and sent a brief, illustrated handout about the project. The following visit was primarily to meet the children and spend some time in the home at a busy time, such as after school or on a Saturday.

A range of child-friendly materials had been designed with the assistance of an illustrator to facilitate the children's involvement. These included brightly-coloured pictures of individual and family activities, sheets to do drawings or write about their family, themselves and their brothers or sisters, and brief illustrated questionnaires about their interests and family experiences. The number of materials used depended on the individual child, although 'Tom', a green squeaky dinosaur who had been employed as research assistant, seemed to be popular with all participants, even some fathers! For a few children with very severe impairments, contact involved spending time getting to know them a little. Observing family activity helped the researchers to understand family interactions, the care needs of the disabled children and how they were being accommodated.

The third visit to families was in order to discuss service support with families and other areas not covered during the first contact. Perceptions and information about the family gathered on previous meetings could also be checked out with the family. Sometimes, further visits were necessary to meet other family members or in order to understand a particularly complex situation.

Reference groups also contributed to the research. Two were recruited at the beginning of the fieldwork: a group of parents in Liverpool; and members of a child development team in Leeds with whom the researcher discussed the main issues for families with two or more severely disabled children. Towards the end of the project these were revisited to discuss and obtain feedback on the main findings of the research, although both had expanded with further parents and professionals. Three further groups of professionals were also

visited for this purpose: a social services children with
disabilities team in York; a combined social services and
Barnardo's team in North East Lincolnshire; and a multi-
agency children's centre in Hull.

The sample of families

The sample of 24 families who participated in the qualitative
part of the project were primarily drawn from the Family
Fund Trust database within the Yorkshire region, although
the South Asian families were recruited via the database of a
voluntary organisation in Manchester, and one family were
approached with the help of the Society for Mucopolysacchar-
ide Diseases.

As much diversity as possible within the sample was aimed
for in order that common key experiences could be identified
across a range of family circumstances and children's
conditions. In order to protect the confidentiality of families
who took part, a detailed profile of each family and their
children has not been included with this report. However,
variation on a number of dimensions was included, in
particular, family composition, family circumstances such as
housing tenure and employment status of parents, area of
residence, an urban/rural mix, and, most importantly,
variation among the disabled children in terms of age, sex
and their impairments, and whether these were the same or
different from those of their brother(s) or sister(s). The
children's conditions included severe learning disabilities,
multiple impairments, Down's syndrome, cerebral palsy,
autism, Fragile X syndrome, brittle bone disease, epilepsy,
Sanfilippo disease, cystic fibrosis, myotonic dystrophy and
muscular neuropathy, deafness and visual impairment. The
majority of children who took part had a learning disability
and many children had more than one impairment. Some of
the children had their life expectancy shortened by their
condition. Five families who took part in the study each had
three disabled children and one had five (four of whom were
adopted).

References

Audit Commission (1994) *Seen but not Heard.* HMSO

Bennett, T, DeLuca, D and Allen, R (1996) 'Families of children with disabilities: positive adaptation across the life cycle', *Social Work in Education,* 18, 1, 31–44

Beresford, B (1994) *Positively Parents: Caring for a severely disabled child.* HMSO

Beresford, B (1995) *Expert Opinions: A national survey of parents caring for a severely disabled child.* The Policy Press

Carpenter, B *(ed)* (1997) *Families in Context: Emerging trends in family support and early intervention.* David Fulton Publishers

Chamba, R and others (1999) *On the Edge: Minority ethnic families caring for a severely disabled child.* The Policy Press

The Children Act 1989. HMSO

Davies, K (1994) 'The tensions between process time and clock time' *Care-Work, Time and Society,* 3, 3, 277–303

Department of Health (1995) *Child Protection: Messages from research.* HMSO

Department of Health (1998) *Quality Protects.* DoH

Department of Health (1999) *Caring about Carers: A national strategy for carers.* DoH

Dobson, B and Middleton, S (1998) *Paying to Care: The cost of childhood disability.* York Publishing Services

Green, J and Murton, F (1993) *Duchenne Muscular Dystrophy: The experiences of 158 families.* Centre for Family Research

Kagan, C, Lewis, S and Heaton, P (1998) *Caring to Work: Accounts of working parents of disabled children.* London: Family Policy Study Centre

Lawton, D (1998) *Complex Numbers: Families with more than one disabled child.* Social Policy Research Unit

McConachie, H (1997) *Do UK Services really Support Parents?* 100 Hours Newsletter

Mirfin-Veitch, B and Bray, A 'Grandparents: Part of the family', *in* Carpenter, B ed (1997) *Families in Context.* David Fulton

Mulderij, K (1996) 'Research into the lifeworld of physically disabled children', *Child: care, health and development,* 22, 5, 311–22

Oldman, C and Beresford, B (1998) *Homes Unfit for Children: Housing, disabled children and their families.* Centre for Housing Policy

Parents at Work (*forthcoming*) *Waving not Drowning.* Parents at Work

Shah, R (1995) *The Silent Minority: Children with disabilities in Asian families.* National Children's Bureau

Shah, R (1997) 'Improving services to Asian families and children with disabilities', *Child: care, health and development,* 23, 1, 41–6

Shared Care UK (1997) *New Horizons: Family-based short breaks for people with autism.* Shared Care UK

Sloper, P and Turner, S (1992) 'Service needs of families of children with severe physical disability' *Child: care, health and development,* 18, 259–82

Social Services Inspectorate (1998) *Removing Barriers for Disabled Children.* Department of Health

Social Services Inspectorate (1999) *Getting Family Support Right: Inspection of the delivery of family support services.* Department of Health

Todd, S and Shearn, J (1996) 'Struggles with time: the careers of parents of adult sons and daughters with learning disabilities', *Disability and Society,* 11, 379–401

Tozer, R (1999) 'Who cares for the carers?', *Community Care,* August 19–25, 22–23

Twigg, J (1989) 'Models of carers' *Journal of Social Policy,* 18, 1, 53–66

Twigg, J, Atkin K and Perring C. (1991) *Carers and Services: A review of research.* HMSO

Wild, N and Rosenbloom, L. (1985) 'Families with more than one handicapped child', *Child: care, health and development* 11, 5, 281–90

Index

A
adaptations in the home 45–6
agencies, coordination between 51–3
analysis
   qualitative 4
   quantitative 3, 18
appointments with professionals 36–7

B
Baker family 1–2
benefits, reliance on 20, 43–5
breaks
   for children 34
   children's views of 42
   for parents 39–42
brothers *see* siblings, non-disabled

C
care, specialised 51
carers, parents as 20–1
Caring about Carers 5
child care 19
Children Act 5
collaborative practice 51–3
'Contact a Family' 24
coordination between agencies 51–3
costs *see* resources

D
demands, disabled children 27–9
Disability Discrimination Act 5–6, 31
Disability Living Allowance 44
disability: questions 2

E
emotional support 35
employment 18–20
equipment and time 29

ethnic families 3–4
   see also South Asians

F
families used for report 64
   see also Baker family
family
   extended 14–15
   going out together 30–1
   important considerations 56–7
   involving in research 4
   outside support 33–46
Family Fund Trust 3, 8, 45
father
   absence 8
   at home 9
flexibility of services 53–4

G
government initiatives 5
grandparents 14–15

H
holidays 45
   see also breaks
home
   adaptations to 45–6
   care 41–2
   help 37–9
housing, suitability 29

I
illness, parents 53–4
Invalid Care Allowance 44
isolation 22–4

J
Joseph Rowntree Foundation 2

K
key workers 48–50

L
legislation 5–6
    see also Children Act; Disability
    Discrimination Act
leisure opportunities 42–3
lifestyles, impact on 18–24
local networks 50
lone parents 8

M
meetings 52–3
mothers, single *see* lone parents

N
networks, local 23–4, 50
non-disabled siblings see siblings, non-
    disabled

P
Pakistani community *see* South Asians
parents
    as full-time carers 20–1
    illness 53–4
    love for children 10–11
    managing 26–31
    new skills 19
    single *see* lone parents
playschemes 42
policy context of report 5–6
process time 27, 37
professionals 48–54
public perception 21–2

Q
qualitative analysis 4
Quality Protects 5
quantitative analysis 3, 18
questions about disability 2

R
racism 24
recommendations of report 56–9
relationship breakdown 8–9
relationships within families 8–17
*Removing Barriers for Disabled
    Children* 6
report
    plan 6

policy context 5–6
recommendations 56–9
research 2–5
    aims 62–4
    involving family 4
    methods 3–4, 62–4
    qualitative 4, 18–19
    quantitative 3, 18
researchers 5
resources 43–5
respite care *see* breaks; terminal
    respite care
reviews 52–3
rural areas, support in 50

S
safety concerns 28
school visits 36
services
    lack of flexibility 53–4
    provided 48–54
    targeted 50–1
short-term care *see* breaks
siblings, non-disabled
    help from 11–14
    and public perception 22
single parents *see* lone parents
sisters *see* siblings, non-disabled
skills, parents 19
South Asians
    family support 15
    parents, isolation of 24
    respite care 41
space needs 30
specialised care 51
support
    emotional 35
    improving 57–9
    outside the family 33–46
    in rural areas 50
    within South Asian families 15

T
targeting services 50–1
tasks 26–7
terminal respite care 41
time and resources 26–31

U
unfairness, feelings of 11